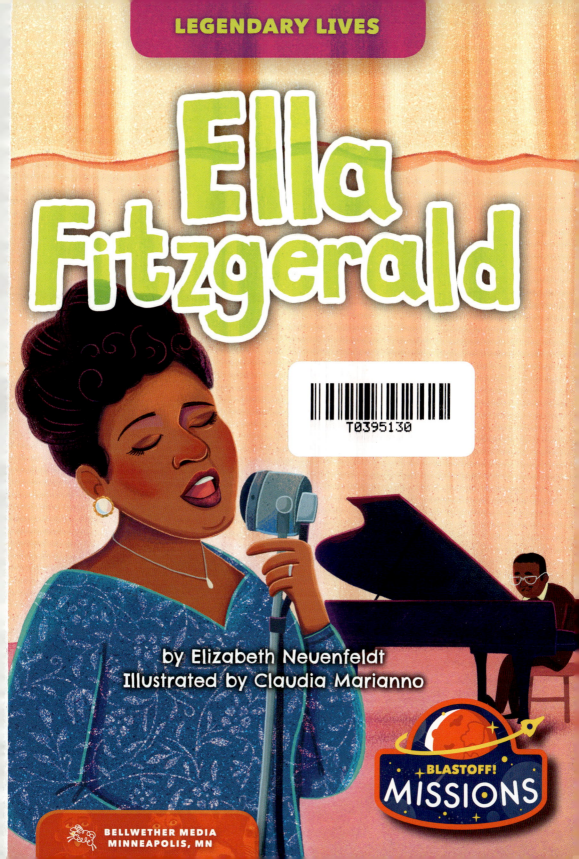

Blastoff! Missions takes you on a learning adventure! Colorful illustrations and exciting narratives highlight cool facts about our world and beyond. Read the mission goals and follow the narrative to gain knowledge, build reading skills, and have fun!

Traditional Nonfiction

Narrative Nonfiction

Blastoff! Universe

MISSION GOALS

> FIND YOUR SIGHT WORDS IN THE BOOK.

> LEARN ABOUT ELLA FITZGERALD'S LIFE.

> LEARN ABOUT HOW ELLA FITZGERALD BECAME AN INSPIRATIONAL JAZZ SINGER.

This edition first published in 2026 by Bellwether Media, Inc.

No part of this publication may be reproduced in whole or in part without written permission of the publisher. For information regarding permission, write to Bellwether Media, Inc., Attention: Permissions Department, 3500 American Blvd W, Suite 150, Bloomington, MN 55431.

Library of Congress Cataloging-in-Publication Data

Names: Neuenfeldt, Elizabeth author | Marianno, Claudia illustrator
Title: Ella Fitzgerald / by Elizabeth Neuenfeldt ; illustrated by Claudia Marianno.
Description: Blastoff! missions. | Minnetonka, MN : Bellwether Media, Inc, 2025. | Series: Legendary lives | Includes bibliographical references and index. | Audience: Ages 5-8 | Audience: Grades 2-3 | Summary: ""Vibrant illustrations accompany information about Ella Fitzgerald. The narrative nonfiction text is intended for students in kindergarten through third grade." -Provided by publisher"-- Provided by publisher.
Identifiers: LCCN 2025018601 (print) | LCCN 2025018602 (ebook) | ISBN 9798893045338 library binding | ISBN 9798893047509 paperback | ISBN 9798893046717 ebook
Subjects: LCSH: Fitzgerald, Ella--Juvenile literature | Jazz musicians--United States--Biography--Juvenile literature | Singers--United States--Biography--Juvenile literature
Classification: LCC ML3930.F5 N48 2025 (print) | LCC ML3930.F5 (ebook) | DDC 782.42165092 [B]--dc23/eng/20250415
LC record available at https://lccn.loc.gov/2025018601
LC ebook record available at https://lccn.loc.gov/2025018602

Text copyright © 2026 by Bellwether Media, Inc. BLASTOFF! MISSIONS and associated logos are trademarks and/or registered trademarks of Bellwether Media, Inc. Bellwether Media is a division of FlutterBee Education Group.

Editor: Rebecca Sabelko   Designer: Andrea Schneider

Printed in the United States of America, North Mankato, MN.

This is **Blastoff Jimmy**! He is here to help you on your mission and share fun facts along the way!

Table of Contents

Meet Ella Fitzgerald	4
Getting into Music	6
Becoming the First Lady of Song	10
Changing the World	20
Glossary	22
To Learn More	23
Beyond the Mission	24
Index	24

Meet Ella Fitzgerald

Getting into Music

It is the 1930s. Young Ella lives in New York. Her mom brings home **jazz** music to play.

Ella loves to sing and dance with the music.

Ella is now 17. She enters a **contest** at the Apollo Theater in **Harlem**. She is nervous to sing. But she wins!

People start to notice Ella's talent.

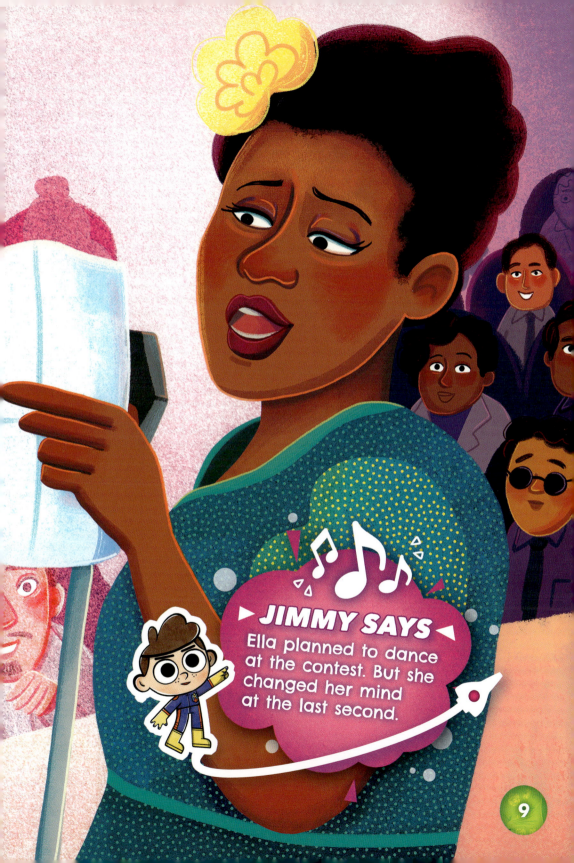

Ella is now part of the Chick Webb **Orchestra**. She helps the group become more popular.

Ella's song "A-Tisket, A-Tasket" is a hit. She is famous!

▶ JIMMY SAYS ◀
"A-Tisket, A-Tasket" came out in 1938. It sold one million copies!

It is now 1948. Ella works with many famous musicians. She starts singing in other countries.

Ella also begins singing on television.

Ella leaves a show in Houston. This city is **segregated**. But her **manager** made the show available to people of color.

JIMMY SAYS

Ella made eight songbook albums. They came out from 1956 to 1964.

Ella is **recording** her songbook albums. They cover music by famous artists.

Ella soon wins her first two **Grammy Awards**. She is the first Black woman to win this award!

Today, Ella receives the National Medal of Arts.

Changing the World

Ella is in her 70s. She creates a **foundation**. It helps children and people in need.

Today, people still listen and sing to her music. Ella continues to **inspire** people!

Ella Fitzgerald Profile

Born

April 25, 1917, in Newport News, Virginia

Died

June 15, 1996

Accomplishments

World-famous singer who won many awards for her skills and talent

Timeline

1934: Ella wins a contest at the Apollo Theater

1948: Ella performs on television for the first time

1956 to 1964: Ella records her songbook albums

1958: Ella wins her first two Grammy Awards

1987: Ella receives the National Medal of Arts

1993: Ella creates the Ella Fitzgerald Charitable Foundation

Glossary

arrest–to place under police control

contest–an event in which people try to win against other people

foundation–a group that gives money in order to do something that helps society

Grammy Awards–awards given to people each year for success in music.

Harlem–a part of New York City that is an important part of Black history

inspire–to give someone an idea about what to do or create

jazz–relating to a kind of American music that has lively rhythms and often has melodies made up by musicians as they play

manager–a person who looks after and makes decisions about another person or group

orchestra–a group of musicians that plays instrumental music together

recording–changing sound into a form that can be listened to at a later time

scats–sings by making up sounds to go with the music

segregated–set apart based on race

To Learn More

AT THE LIBRARY

Becker, Trudy. *Jazz*. Mendota Heights, Minn.: Focus Readers, 2025.

Kirkfield, Vivian. *Making Their Voices Heard: The Inspiring Friendship of Ella Fitzgerald and Marilyn Monroe*. New York, N.Y.: Little Bee Books, 2020.

Rathburn, Betsy. *John Lewis*. Minneapolis, Minn.: Bellwether Media, 2025.

ON THE WEB

FACTSURFER

Factsurfer.com gives you a safe, fun way to find more information.

1. Go to www.factsurfer.com.

2. Enter "Ella Fitzgerald" into the search box and click 🔍.

3. Select your book cover to see a list of related content.

BEYOND THE MISSION

> WHAT FACT FROM THE BOOK DO YOU THINK WAS THE MOST INTERESTING?

> THINK ABOUT A PERSON WHO INSPIRES YOU. WHAT DO THEY INSPIRE YOU TO ACHIEVE?

> LISTEN TO SOME OF ELLA'S RECORDINGS. ARE THERE ANY SONGS YOU LIKE? WHY OR WHY NOT?

Index

Apollo Theater, 8
arrest, 15
Chick Webb
  Orchestra, 11
contest, 8, 9
dance, 7, 9
foundation, 20
Grammy Awards, 17
Harlem, 8
Houston, 14
jazz music, 7
manager, 14
mom, 7

National Medal of Arts, 18, 19
New York, 7
nickname, 5
police, 15
profile, 21
scats, 5
segregated, 14
sings, 5, 7, 8, 13, 15, 20
song, 11
songbook albums, 17
stage, 5
television, 13